MARTIN LUTHER

by

JOHN BROOME

GOSPEL STANDARD TRUST PUBLICATIONS
1994

12(b) Roundwood Lane, Harpenden,
Herts. AL5 3DD, England

MARTIN LUTHER

LUTHER was born in 1483 in the Thuringian Forest area of Germany at Eisleben. His father was a miner, though not an uneducated man. He sent his son to school at Magdeburg and Eisenach. At Eisenach Luther found a good home with Ursula Cotta, wife of one of the burghers of the town. This was a great contrast to the condition of many boys at school, who regularly in Germany went about begging for their food, which in fact Luther had had to do himself at Magdeburg. In 1501 his father sent him to Erfurt University. (The area in which he lived and was educated is now in the Eastern Zone of Germany). He worked here for two years on Classics and Theology; the theology of men like Thomas Aquinas. One day he found a Bible on the shelves of the Library—a Latin Vulgate Bible. He had never seen one before. He read first how Samuel was called of God, and given to the Lord by his mother. Day after day he returned to read the Bible. It was the year 1503, a year marked in his life as that in which he obtained his B.A.

Too much study brought on a serious illness, but he recovered and was left with an impression that God had spared his life for a purpose. In 1505 he took his M.A. His intention at this stage in his career was to become a lawyer. In the summer of this year he went to visit his parents and on the return journey to Erfurt was caught in a severe thunderstorm, lightning striking the ground very near to him. Death seemed close and in the intensity of the moment he vowed that if spared he would devote his life to God. With his prospects in life—he was one of the most brilliant students of his University—it meant an immense sacrifice to go into a monastery, for that was what he considered service to God entailed. On 17th August, 1505 he kept his vow and entered the monastery of the Augustinian Hermits at Erfurt. Here he experienced many hardships; was called on to do the most menial tasks and generally devote himself to the monastic life. Since the thunderstorm, he had been especially concerned about his soul's welfare for eternity, and felt the need of preparation in the removal of guilt between him and God. He hoped in the quiet cloisters he would find this peace of conscience and live near to heaven. He proved himself mistaken, for his burden increased there. During his many exercises of soul he met John Staupitz, Vicar-General of the Augustinian Order, who said to him, "It is not in vain that God exercises you in so many conflicts. You will see that He will employ you as His servant for great purposes. Let the study of the Scriptures be your favourite occupation." The Vicar-General could have hardly realised 'the great purposes' or he might not have uttered such words. His advice to read the Scriptures was certainly unusual, coming from a high dignitary of the Roman Catholic Church at that time.

Luther spent much of his time in the monastery reading the works of St. Augustine; he liked especially Augustine on 'the Psalms'. He found a chained Bible in the monastery which he read regularly. He began a study of the Bible in its Greek and Hebrew originals, which enabled him later to translate it into German. But forgiveness he felt unable to find until taken ill, and very seriously ill, one of the old monks repeated to him the words of the Apostle's Creed, "I believe in the forgiveness of sins." These words were blessed to his soul in such a manner that he was, there and then, enabled by the operation of the Holy Spirit to powerfully believe that his own sins had been forgiven by the Lord Jesus Christ on Calvary. Roman Catholicism was destroyed in his soul. Salvation was for him no longer a question of how holy he could make himself. The great doctrine always associated with him came before him—salvation was by faith alone in the Lord Jesus, and not of works. No cloisters to avoid a sinful world, no indulgences or any other means could atone for sin. Luther learnt that Christ loved him and had died for him.

After two years in the monastery, in May 1507 he was ordained a priest. He had not yet been led to see the errors of the Roman Catholic priesthood, but long before he died he

MARTIN LUTHER

realised that he received no power for his life's work from that ordination. After one more year in the monastery, he was sent at the suggestion of John Staupitz to lecture in the University of Wittemberg, founded in 1502 by the Elector of Saxony. He was to lecture in scholastic philosophy. This subject was far from what he wanted and he was soon transferred to lecture in theology, which enabled him to start on his chosen subject, scriptural exposition. He began his lectures with the Epistle of Paul to the Romans. The Bible, so long a closed book in Germany, was once again in Luther's hands to find its rightful place in University teaching and be expounded faithfully by a man who loved it and held it in reverence. Would that such a situation might again come about in this country in our own Universities where modernism has so infiltrated Biblical studies that, in a different way, the Bible is almost as closed a book as it was in Luther's day, being relegated to a more than secondary place among the sources of wisdom.

Having settled in the University, Staupitz proposed to Luther that he should not confine his teaching to University students, but go outside the University and preach in public. In the public square of Wittemberg was an old wooden church, thirty feet long and twenty feet wide. In it was an old wooden pulpit. Here Luther started his public ministry and broke the silence of centuries in Germany with the Gospel. He preached from his heart and his utterances came with power, the power of the Holy Spirit speaking through him to the hearts of his countrymen. Such preaching had not been heard in Germany for years. Soon the Church was overcrowded and the Town Council of Wittemberg called him to be their preacher and use the Parish Church. Powerful preaching was at the root of the Reformation—it always has been so; the Lord has used His servants, raised and equipped, for His divine purposes, and Luther was no exception to this. He was a man raised and equipped of God to lighten the darkness of 'Medieval Christendom.'

But he had one more lesson to learn before he was fully equipped. Wylie remarks, "In his cell at Erfurt he had been shown the sinfulness of his own heart . . . At Rome he must be shown the vileness of the Church which he still regarded as the Church of Christ." In 1510 he was sent to Rome by the Augustinian Order. Why he went hardly concerns us—it was a conflict between the German Augustinians and the Papacy. But what does concern us is the effect that the journey had on Luther. Travelling across the Alps he came to stay at a monastery in Northern Italy, a splendid wealthy place, beautifully furnished and with much rich food. Compared with the German monasteries this was luxurious and it struck Luther as very out of keeping with the concept he had of monastic life. He went forward to Rome and there he received a rude awakening. Far from being the Holy City he had imagined, the centre of the Christian Church, he found it to be the very centre of godlessness and scepticism, not only among the ordinary people but among the clergy themselves and even among the Church dignitaries. While in Rome he climbed the Holy Stairs, said to have been miraculously transported from Jerusalem by angels, and which, if climbed on one's knees, according to the Church, one received fifteen years indulgence from purgatory. While engaged in the act the Lord spoke to his heart the words, "The just shall live by his faith," and the words came with such power that he felt it was the voice of God to him. He started to his feet in amazement. He saw at once that the Church's indulgence was limited, whereas Christ's forgiveness procured at Calvary was for ever. From this day in the 'Holy City' he learnt the lesson of a lifetime. God had used his journey to Rome to teach him the great doctrine of Justification by Faith, and it was burnt into his very soul. He saw it as he had never seen it before and God was his teacher and not man. It was a doctrine which the Roman Church had lost for many centuries and had relied instead on salvation by works. Luther said afterwards that he would not have missed his journey to Rome 'for an hundred thousand florins.' He was not there for more than a few weeks, but in that time the seeds of the Reformation were sown in his heart. He was to preach against and expose the Roman Catholic Church out of a practical acquaintance in his own heart of its evils and abuses. His eyes had been opened to the truth of the Gospel by the Holy Spirit in a way they might not otherwise have been had he never visited Rome.

And so he returned to Germany. There he was made a Doctor of Divinity at Wittemberg University in October 1512 and this further opened up the way for him to teach and expound the Scriptures; also he continued to preach in the City Church. Over the years that followed from 1512-1517, he was learning for himself and sowing the seed. In 1516 he was commissioned to visit a large number of monasteries in the Thuringian area of Germany and took the opportunity of spreading the truth as the Lord had taught him it. In 1517 the Pope, who wanted money to build and improve Rome and her Churches, decided to issue a special Papal indulgence. The distribution of this and collection of the resulting finances in Germany fell to the lot of Friar Tetzel. He set out to travel round Germany and in the year 1517 he came to Juterbock, four miles from Wittemberg. Such blatant teaching of salvation by works, even to the extent of the use of such language as, "At the very instant that the money rattles in the bottom of the chest, the soul (of your dead relative) escapes from purgatory and flies liberated to heaven," roused Luther. He solemnly warned his students and congregation that there was no salvation without repentance. God, he said, demands a satisfaction for sin, but not from the sinner and it certainly cannot be bought in the form of a Papal pardon or indulgence. Tetzel soon heard of Luther's condemnation of his work and lit a fire in the market-place of Juterbock saying that in such a fire the Pope burnt heretics.

Luther still could not believe that the Pope was party to such deception as Tetzel preached. He wrote to the Archbishop of Mainz asking him to stop Tetzel. He little knew that it was this Archbishop who had authorised Tetzel to carry on his sale of indulgences in Germany. In the University of Wittemberg Luther condemned the scandal. The issue was salvation through the preaching of the Gospel or salvation through indulgences; salvation by grace or salvation by works.

THE REFORMERS

Tetzel went on with his sale and Luther considered how best to attack him. All-Saints Day was 1st November. At Wittemberg, the Elector of Saxony had recently built himself a Castle Church and collected numerous relics to put in it. These in gold and jewelled settings were displayed on All-Saints Day to crowds of spectators who came to earn an indulgence by a visit to the relics. On the previous day, 31st October, at noon, when the streets of Wittemberg were full of the crowds assembling for the following day, Luther went to the Castle Church and boldly nailed to its door a document containing ninety-five propositions (Theses) on indulgences. A few extracts will show the sort of thing that these famous "95 Theses" contained.

VI. The Pope cannot remit any condemnation but can only declare and confirm the remission that God Himself has given . . .

XXI. The sellers of indulgences are in error when they say that by the Papal indulgence a man is delivered from every punishment and is saved.

XXXVII. Every true Christian, dead or living, is a partaker of all the blessings of Christ or of the Church, by the gift of God and without any letter of indulgence.

LII. To hope to be saved by indulgences is a lying and an empty hope, although even the seller of indulgences, nay even the Pope himself, should pledge their souls to guarantee it.

LIII. They are the enemies of the Pope and Jesus Christ who, by reason of the preaching of indulgences, forbid the preaching of the Word of God.

LXII. The true and precious treasure of the Church is the Holy Gospel of the glory and grace of God.

It is clear from these propositions that Luther still recognised the Roman Catholic Church as the centre of Christianity, though corrupt. He really was quite ignorant of its machinations, even after his visit to Rome in 1510, and could not believe initially in 1517 that it needed more than thoroughly reforming. But a proposition like LXII shows that if he had not yet a clear view of the system in which he had

MARTIN LUTHER

been nurtured, he was quite clear on the system to which the Lord was leading him, and the central feature of that system was its reverence for and acceptance of the authority of the Scriptures and their revelation of the Gospel. As Wylie points out, Luther had taken the mightiest of all the powers of the Church, the power of pardoning sin and so saving men's souls, and given it back to God. The intention behind his Theses was that they should form the basis for a debate in the University on All-Saints Day. But though he offered to defend them, no-one was prepared to oppose him. Instead a debate of a different kind ensued—in the minds of the men, the pilgrims to Wittemberg who had come from the surrounding parts of Germany, and who took away as well as their indulgence, printed copies of Luther's Theses and discussed them on their journey home. Such was the means used of spreading the seeds of the Reformation in its earliest beginnings—not a debate of one day in Wittemberg, but a continuing debate which is still in progress and will, God willing, last as long as the Christian Church on earth. The big question in 1517 was—is what Luther says true? If so then the infallible Church was no longer infallible and there must be some major discrepancy between it and the Scriptures.

In a fortnight Luther's Theses were distributed all over Germany. Then they were translated into Dutch and Spanish and circulated in those countries. In a month they were all round Europe. In four weeks Luther's name was a household word in Europe. In Universities and monasteries, in the market place and the palace, even in the Vatican itself where the Pope read them, they were the centre of discussion. Luther's lamp of truth was indeed set on a hill and no-one was more surprised than Luther at the effect of his attack. Tetzel had by now moved on to Frankfort-on-Oder, where he publicly burnt a copy of the Theses and produced some of his own in which he re-affirmed the authority of the Roman Catholic Church as opposed to the authority of the Bible. Other antagonists took up Tetzel's side, among whom was a famous scholar of Ingolstadt, Dr. Eck. He accused Luther of spreading the "Bohemian poison", a reference to Huss.

In April 1518, Luther went to a meeting of the Augustinian Order at Heidelberg and there defended his case. Many who had come from various monasteries in Germany were very impressed by his defence, especially his constant reference to Scripture, and they returned to their monasteries with matter for thought. Some of the monks were chaplains to the princely rulers of the small states into which Germany was divided at that time, and they took back ideas for discussion with their masters.

In August 1518 the Pope was roused to a sense of the danger by the Emperor of Germany, Maximilian, and ordered Luther to come to Rome. Later he changed his mind and decided that Cardinal Cajetan would judge the case of heresy in Germany and Luther was ordered to go to Augsburg and appear before the Cardinal there. A few days before he left, a new Professor arrived at Wittemberg University to take the Chair of Greek. This was Philip Melanchthon, who was to be a fellow Reformer and companion to Luther, just at a time when he was standing alone and under attack. Melanchthon had come from Heidelberg University, where he had taken his degree. Both men had come from lowly origins—Luther the son of a miner, Melanchthon the son of a master armourer. This was true of the other Reformers. Calvin was the grandson of a cooper of Picardy in France, Knox was the son of a Scottish burgess, Zwingli was born in a shepherd's cottage in the Swiss Alps. As in His day on earth, the Lord chose His disciples of the Reformation from such humble homes as His own at Nazareth. But, as with Paul, he made use of their ability in combating the false theology of the Roman Catholic Church.

So Luther set out for Augsburg rather like Huss to Constance, not certain whether he would return alive to Wittemberg or die at the stake, but with the same confidence in God that Paul had on his last journey back to Jerusalem, "ready not to be bound only, but also to die for the name of the Lord Jesus." Unlike Huss, initially Luther had no safe-conduct, and many seriously doubted the outcome of his examination before the Cardinal. He arrived at Augsburg after a journey of several hundred miles on foot, on 7th October. It was not

MARTIN LUTHER

quite a year since he had posted his Theses on the door of the Castle Church at Wittemberg and now he was being judged for it by the Roman Catholic Church. Cardinal Cajetan wanted one thing only—submission—recantation. If Luther refused that, he intended to send him to Rome bound. In Augsburg Luther was encouraged to find that even to this place his doctrines had spread; and it was one of the most important cities in the German Empire. Before going into the presence of the Cardinal his friends helped him to obtain a safe-conduct from the Emperor Maximilian. Then Luther went to defend his cause. Two of his Theses were selected as being the centre of his heresy—VII, in which he had denied that the Sacrament had any profit unless mixed with faith on the part of the partaker, and LVIII, in which he had denied that the merits of Christ formed any part of that treasure from which the Pope granted indulgences to the 'faithful'. On Cajetan asking Luther to recant on these two issues, Luther asked to be shown from Scripture where they were in error. Cajetan replied by quoting the decrees of the Church. Luther again returned to Scripture only to be told that the Pope was the supreme authority in such matters and was above Scripture and Councils of the Church. Unable to come to any agreement, Cajetan gave Luther an opportunity to go away and reconsider the matter.

Luther returned next day and offered to submit his Theses to the judgement of the Imperial Universities of Basle, Fribourg and Louvain, and if necessary also to the University of Paris. Cajetan was embarrassed at this for it was quite likely that these Universities were similarly affected with Reformed views as was Wittemberg. Again he asked Luther to go away and this time to put his case in writing. When he returned the third time, Luther read a long statement quoting Augustine, and other Christian Fathers and the Scriptures. Cajetan was furious and called it 'mere words'. He agreed however to send it to Rome to be examined. Once more he asked Luther to recant and when he refused he offered him a safe-conduct to go to Rome and be tried there. Luther refused the offer knowing the value of Vatican safe-conducts and remembering that good-faith was not to be kept with heretics according to the Council of Constance's treatment of Huss. He was astonished at the weakness of Cajetan in his defence of the Roman Catholic position. If this was one of the Pope's great theologians who refused to argue from Scripture and appeared to be unable to do so, what were the rest like at Rome? Cajetan ordered Luther "to be gone and see his face no more, unless he changed his mind," and sensing danger, Luther wrote to the Cardinal a letter and receiving no reply, at dawn on 20th October he left Augsburg quietly on horse. His escape was none too soon. The Cardinal's orders were to arrest him if he refused to recant. Luther reached Wittemberg safely on 31st October, the anniversary of his posting-up of the Theses.

Although Cajetan had failed to obtain a recantation from Luther, the Pope was not willing to excommunicate him at once. He was not the first member of the Roman Catholic Church who had disagreed with the Pope and it was expected in Rome that the trouble might die down and eventually disappear. However the Pope decided to try and appease the Elector of Saxony in whose State Wittemberg was, and get him to hand Luther over for trial. So a Papal Envoy, Charles Miltitz, was sent to Germany with a "golden rose" for the Elector of Saxony. This was a special mark of the Pope's favour and much coveted by the princes of Europe. On his journey Miltitz was amazed to discover how the question of the attack of the German monk on the Pope occupied the discussions of the Germans. Wherever he went he met it, the majority favouring Luther's side. The Elector of Saxony was not too pleased to see Miltitz. He was far enough away from Rome to value what freedom he possessed and resent political interference from the Pope. He was not a heretic nor anywhere approaching it, but he had a mind of his own and had not much love for Italian ecclesiastics. Miltitz then turned his attention to Luther. He tried out the subtle art of diplomacy. He had several interviews with Luther between 4-6th January, 1519, in which he admitted that Tetzel had been wrong and also the Archbishop of Mainz, who had supported him. But he maintained that it was not the doctrine of indulgences that was wrong, only their abuse. He asked

Luther to confess to his error in attacking indulgences. But Luther refused and pointed out that the blame rested squarely on the shoulders of the Pope. After the interviews Miltitz persuaded Luther to agree not to attack the Pope in public so long as the Pope did not attack him. In other words the conflict was to be halted on both sides and nothing controversial published or said. This was a subtle and very dangerous manoeuvre, for the Reformation gained all by spreading the truth and here Luther was silenced, except in preaching and lecturing at Wittemberg. By doing this Miltitz hoped that the matter would die out and gradually disaffected Roman Catholics would forget Luther and peace and unity would return to the Church.

Then on 12th January, 1519 the Emperor of Germany, Maximilian, died and the new Emperor was not elected until 28th June that year. During this period the Regency was in the hands of the Elector of Saxony, in fact the Regency continued until the new Emperor, Charles V, was crowned at Aix-la-Chapelle on 23rd October, 1520. This was a period of grace for Luther, as the Pope could not act against him until the political affairs of Germany were settled and a new Emperor chosen. All that time Luther was able to shelter under the protection of the Elector of Saxony who was not unfavourable to his cause. In June 1519 the Papacy broke its truce with Luther. Dr. Eck, the Chancellor of Ingolstadt University, a leading debater and defender of the Roman Catholic Church, issued Thirteen Theses, attacking Luther's teaching and Luther now felt free from his obligation to Miltitz. Eck offered the Reformers an open challenge in public debate, to defend their position and they accepted to come to Leipzig for the debate. They arrived on 24th June; Eck had arrived three days before and received a civic welcome. The city took a serious interest in something that was now of great public concern. German princes and nobility were present and the atmosphere was far from that of a mere academic discussion in a University Hall. Tables were provided for clerks who were to record the debate. The Hall was full of spectators. It lasted from 4-14th July, 1519. The questions discussed were those which have always divided the Protestant and Roman Catholic Churches. It showed the Reformers just how deep the differences were between the two sides. Melanchthon, Luther's fellow reformer, was present, also another lesser known theologian, Carlstadt, Archdeacon of Wittemberg Cathedral, a supporter of Luther.

Carlstadt spoke first in defence of the truth. The controversy centred on a man's will. The proposition defended by Carlstadt was, "Man's will before his conversion can perform no good work. Every good work comes entirely and exclusively from God, who gives to man first the will to do and then the power to accomplish". The Reformers looked back to Augustine and Paul ("the carnal mind is enmity against God") in defence of their proposition. It was a truth which had been lost sight of in the Roman Catholic Church for many generations. Paul had said, "It is God that worketh in you both to will and to do of his good pleasure," and had spoken of men being, "alienated from the life of God through the ignorance that is in them." From this there followed the evangelical truth, "Ye must be born again." "That which is born of the flesh is flesh, that which is born of the Spirit is Spirit." Eck, for the Roman Catholic Church, while admitting that man was a fallen creature, limited the extent of that fall and maintained that he could do something towards his own salvation. In fact he could choose holiness if he wished, and while still unconverted could do acts which had merit, and God would reward these works done in man's own strength with grace, to do what was still needed towards the perfecting of his own salvation. Luther and Carlstadt fought for the truth, "By grace are ye saved; through faith, and that not of yourself, it is the gift of God." This was salvation by grace to the entire exclusion of any human merit. The Roman Catholic Church, while recognising God's grace in salvation, maintained that salvation began in man's own effort and good works, and that these continued in his life, and were to be considered as meritorious in his salvation; that is, salvation by grace and works. To Luther works were also essential, "By their fruits ye shall know them," but the works of a true believer were, as he saw it, an act of obedience; "if ye love me, keep my commandments," and they in no way acted meritoriously in salvation. Luther firmly believed that, "Faith without works is dead," but saw the truth of Ephesians 3.8. "By *grace* are ye *saved,* through faith . . . " So the controversy centred around one point as it always has and always will in this conflict of Protestantism and Roman Catholicism, when the Protestantism is soundly based on truly Reformed doctrine; Free-will being the doctrine of the Roman Catholic Church and Free Grace that of the Protestant Church. The question was, "Has the will power to choose and do was is *spiritually* good?" Eck suggested that under the Reformers' scheme of things, man was reduced to a mere log or stone. He forgot how the Scriptures described the matter, *"dead* in trespasses and sins."

Then the discussion turned on the supremacy of the Pope, and Luther and Eck argued on the text, "Thou art Peter, and upon this rock I will build my church." Luther put the Reformed view, that the rock was Christ Himself, Peter confirming what he understood Jesus to mean in his Epistle (1 Pet. 2.6), where under divine inspiration, he attributed the fulfilment of Isaiah 28.16 — "Behold I lay in Sion a chief corner stone", as a reference to Christ. Luther pointed to his interpretation as being that of the early Christian leaders, such as Augustine of Hippo. Eck realised that he was losing and so he turned to raise prejudice against Luther — he accused him of being "a patron of the heresies of Wycliffe and Huss." Luther was bold. He said he strongly disagreed with schism in the Church, but he found that some of the articles of Huss, condemned by the Council of Constance, were plainly evangelical and Christian. In making this stand he not only condemned the Popes, but also the Councils of the Church, and took Protestantism to its final resting place for authority, the Scriptures. This stand lost Luther some of his supporters among the German nobility, who lived in fear of being branded heretics; but it brought out another clear dividing line between Protestant and Roman Catholics, the sole authority of Scripture, and it brought Luther many allies among the students of Leipzig University who, after this debate, moved in large numbers to Wittenberg. Also many of Luther's friends, especially Melanchthon, came to have a clearer understanding of the truth through listening to the debate, and were later useful in the Lord's work in the Reformation. Luther described his work as being to clear the ground and Melanchthon's to till and plant it. In this 'Leipzig Disputation' the two men were brought closely together in understanding of the great truths of the Reformation. Both sides claimed the victory, though actually no differences were resolved nor could be. For Luther it was a place where he could propagate the truth and this to him was victory, even if Eck did not concede he was right. The two sides were arguing from fundamentally differing positions — Luther basing his arguments on Scripture alone, and Eck on Scripture plus Church traditions and decrees of Popes and Councils. The whole issue was and ever will be unresolvable however much our present generation of so-called 'Protestants' think they can find a solution.

After the Leipzig Disputation with Eck in July 1519, the next event of importance was Luther's publication in September of his famous "Commentary on Galatians". It contained the essence of his understanding of the doctrine of justification by faith and was a manual of the Reformation. It has been reprinted in numerous editions since and is still in print in this country today, and obtainable at any Christian Bookshop. Readers would find it profitable to obtain a copy and read such a book which contains the freshness of the first attack on Roman Catholic errors, especially as many are not conscious today of the tremendous gulf which still divides Roman Catholicism and Protestantism; and such teaching would be an asset in discussion with present day Roman Catholics and a useful book to lend to such people.

Early in 1520 Dr. Eck went to Rome to get Luther excommunicated and succeeded. The decree was published in Rome on 15th June. A letter was sent by the Pope to the Elector of Saxony ordering him to stamp out Luther's heresy. The reaction of the Elector was to resolve to protect Luther. He still had an important say in the political affairs of Germany until Charles V was crowned Emperor in October 1520 and was not prepared to sacrifice Luther to the Pope's anger without a fair trial. Luther realised how precarious his position was humanly speaking, and in August 1520 he published his "Appeal to the Emperor and German Nobles." In it he outlined the slavery, spiritual and political, which the Papal supremacy had produced in Germany and Europe. Priests were immune from civil law and the Church had its own ecclesiastical courts. He condemned the whole system as one of tyranny, and robbery resulting in the destruction of body and soul. He suggested that the German rulers should resist the Pope by refusing to pay taxes and build monasteries. He also suggested that priests be allowed to marry. The work was a real attack on the Roman Catholic Church and gave to the Reformation in Germany a national appeal. The Reformation was now turning from being a struggle between Luther and the Pope, to be fought out in Germany itself, with Charles V acting as the Pope's agent dealing with a problem in his own Empire, which was as much religious as political, in that it was of such dimensions that it was beginning to form a real dividing issue among the German princes, some of whom supported Luther and some the Pope. In this context the next step for Luther was that he would have to appear before the Emperor and German princes to justify his beliefs.

In the meantime, before that event took place early in 1521, he continued to expose the rottenness of the Catholic Church and wrote his pamphlet "On the Babylonish Captivity of the Church," which was published in October 1520. In it he portrayed the Papacy as the centre of error and evil. The Papal Bull of excommunication arrived at Wittemberg in October 1520. As the Bull was brought to Germany in the hands of Dr. Eck and Aleander, his friend, Luther's books were burnt in public in various cities. Luther replied by burning the Papal Bull in public at Wittemberg on 10th December, 1520 in the presence of the University Doctors and students. There was popular acclaim for this act in Wittemberg and throughout Germany. It was an act of national defiance of the Papacy. Charles V had been crowned Emperor on 23rd October and had at once left Aix-la-Chapelle for Worms (due to the fact that the plague was raging in Aix-la-Chapelle) where he proposed to hold his first Imperial Diet (Parliament). Aleander, the Pope's envoy, was waiting to persuade Charles to act against Luther. Tetzel, Cajetan, Miltitz and Eck had all failed to stop him spreading the truth and the Papal Bull had not been put into operation fully; Luther was still alive. Aleander approached the Elector of Saxony—only to be told that *he* wanted justice done. No-one so far as he knew, had yet proved justly that Luther was in the wrong. Luther must be brought before a tribunal of impartial judges, he suggested. This all pointed to Luther appearing before the Diet about to be held at Worms. Aleander saw a great danger to the Roman Catholic Church in this—in that it would give Luther and his cause public recognition and a public hearing and spread 'the heresy' even further. If possible the Roman Catholic Church wished to stop Luther having any more publicity for spreading the truth. As the Elector of Saxony was the most powerful prince in Germany and as Charles V owed his election as Emperor of Germany to him (the Elector had refused to be elected Emperor himself) Charles had to conciliate him. But Charles also had to keep on the right side of the Pope. Charles was just on the verge of war with France. He could use the request of the Pope to deal with Luther as a bribe for the Pope's support in his war against France. If the Pope came in on his side he would deal with Luther, if not, he would leave Luther free.

The Diet of Worms opened on 28th January, 1521. The Pope agreed to support Charles against France and the Emperor undertook to deal with Luther. A second Bull had been issued on 3rd January, 1521. The first had excommunicated Luther allowing him a certain period to recant—this one was final and complete; there were no conditions. The Emperor now prepared to fulfil his part and as the most powerful monarch in Europe, Emperor of Germany and King of Spain, with vast armies at his disposal, though only a lad of nineteen or twenty, he set out to exterminate the Lutheran heresy. But he found that, on consulting the princes of Germany, though most of them cared little for Luther, they wanted to maintain their privileges, and one of these was not to give in to the Papacy too quickly. So what Aleander had feared happened. The princes asked to be allowed to hear Luther for themselves defend his case before the Imperial Diet at Worms. So, under a safe-conduct, Luther was invited on the 6th March, 1521 to appear before the Diet. He arrived at Worms from Wittemberg on 16th April and appeared before the august Assembly of German princes and nobles on 17th and 18th. It is said that it was on this long journey that he composed his famous hymn,

> A mighty fortress is our God,
> Ein feste Burg ist unser Gott

at Oppenheim on 14th April, just before he reached Worms on the 16th. Great crowds gathered in the streets to welcome him as he entered the city. He appeared the following day—the 17th—before the Emperor at four in the afternoon.

It was a tremendous ordeal for Luther to have to appear before such an assembly. He spent most of that day in prayer. On appearing before the Diet, he was addressed by Dr. Eck, who asked him to own the authorship of his books, which they had there on a table and to retract the opinions expressed in them. Luther owned to their authorship after the titles had been read to him, but he refused to retract his opinions, saying that "the question concerned the salvation of souls" and was too serious to reply to without reflection. The Diet considered his request and allowed him a day's grace. He must appear at the same time on the following day and give his answer. In the morning of the next day Luther felt a horror of darkness descend on his soul, such were his fears; but by the time he had to return to answer before the Emperor the Lord had restored peace and calm to his soul and, as Melanchthon said, when he did appear before the Emperor, "He was more than himself." At this moment Luther was so conscious that the whole cause rested on him, and he so felt his utter insufficiency for it, that he was driven to cast his whole burden on the Lord and the Lord visibly sustained him. It was a fact that he was contending with the whole might of the Roman Catholic Church and the huge political forces of the Emperor of Germany; and what man would not have wilted in such a contest, especially as it was in public before the eyes of the whole German nation in its Parliamentary Assembly? Luther felt that if he, in nervous agitation, was unable to present his case clearly there, then all would mock his cause and he would bring dishonour on the Lord's Name. But another had gone this way before him and stood before Kings and Emperors, and the Lord had upheld His servant Paul, and so He would His servant Luther, and by increasing the magnitude of the opposition, and bringing His servant to feel his utter need, He would manifest His power over all the opposition of man, bring about a remarkable victory and take all the glory for it to Himself.

So Luther returned to present his final answer. He divided his writings, he said, into three categories. The first were merely exposition of the Scripture, and no-one disagreed with these. In the second group he had attacked the corruption, abuses and oppression of the Papacy, and none could disagree that much of what he said was true. In the third group he had attacked particular people who supported the errors and abuses. He confessed to having treated them perhaps harshly, but if so the truth remained that he was in the right and they were in error. As a man he confessed he was liable to mistake. If they would show him clearly any error in his works, he would admit it. He warned the rulers present of a judgement to come in which all would be on trial. He pointed to the great fallen Empires of Babylon, Egypt and Nineveh. Then, after a short rest, Luther repeated all he had said in Latin (previously he had been speaking in German) for the sake of Charles V who did not understand German very well. In all Luther spoke for two hours. The princes felt that if they had come to judge Luther, in fact he had turned the scales on them and reproved them with an extraordinary authority, which they had to fall before and acknowledge.

When he had finished Dr. Eck rose and accused Luther of not answering the question. He was not there to bring in question the authority of Councils of the Church, but merely to state whether he would or would not retract his error. The authority of the Roman Catholic Church was above question! To this Luther replied, "I will give you an answer—it is this. I cannot submit my faith either to the Pope or the Councils, because it is clear as day that they have frequently erred and contradicted each other. Unless therefore I am convinced by the testimony of Scripture or on plain and clear grounds of reason, so that conscience shall bind me to make acknowledgement of error, *I cannot and will not retract,* for it is neither safe nor wise to do anything contrary to conscience." Then, looking round the Assembly, he said, "Here I stand. I can do no other. May God help me. Amen." The Assembly was moved to a murmur of applause, as much as was permissible in the presence of the Emperor. The Roman Catholic party was horrified. The news of this was bound to spread throughout the German Empire and all over Europe. Luther was asked to withdraw while the Assembly debated. A real crisis was now on hand. He was recalled and again asked to retract. He said, he had no other answer to give them than that which he had already given. He had won. No martyr's stake could now silence the truth or heal the great divide between truth and error.

From the time of the Diet of Worms in 1521, the Reformation began to take a turn outside the bounds of the German Empire and spread over Europe. The Diet marks the beginning of this expansion of the movement. The princes in the Diet were impressed by Luther's firmness, yet his respect shown to them. The Elector of Saxony was very pleased with Luther's fearless yet respectful bearing before the Emperor and Assembly. The aged Duke of Brunswick, a Papal member of the Diet, sent a servant to Luther's lodgings with a silver tankard of beer immediately after the Diet. Luther felt it was remarkable coming from such a man just after he had passed through such an ordeal—it was truly "a cup of cold water offered in the Lord's name." This prince, when dying shortly afterwards, called for the Bible to be read to him and the page read those words, "Whosoever shall give you a cup of water to drink in my name, because ye belong to Christ, verily, I say unto you, he shall not lose his reward." From this time many of the princes of Germany became firm friends of Luther and the Reformation. Some openly confessed their change of position at the time. The Elector of

Saxony was firmly resolved to protect Luther, but realised that it would be best if it was done in the least visible way. So while doing all he could to help Luther, he avoided meeting him personally.

The Papal party now persuaded the Emperor to set in motion proceedings to exterminate by all means possible Luther and his heresy. But he would not do this without the consent of the princes and when the matter was raised in the Diet on the following day, two sides became clearly visible; those who supported the Papacy, desiring to burn Luther and scatter his ashes in the Rhine; and those who defended the safe-conduct granted to him, being horrified at such treachery and demanding that it be honoured. The violation of the safe-conduct granted to Huss and then dishonoured was recalled and the Elector of the Palatinate said that, "calamity has never ceased to pursue Germany" for that act of treachery. It should not be repeated. Even Roman Catholic princes, firm in their Catholicism, supported the upholding of the safe-conduct. Had Luther been sacrificed there was every possibility of civil war in Germany at once, such was the strength of the hold of Reformation truths in Germany by 1521. So the Diet rejected the idea of burning Luther. Also Charles V, on the verge of war with France, could not afford to unleash civil war in Germany.

The result was that on 26th April Luther left Worms in peace, surrounded by twenty gentlemen on horseback and followed by large crowds who had come to see this remarkable man. His journey across Germany back north to Wittemberg was amid popular demonstrations, even more enthusiastic than his journey south. A few days after he left the Emperor issued an Edict against him, commanding that as soon as his safe-conduct expired he was to be captured and bound by anyone who found him and sent to the Emperor. The Edict was ratified by a minority group of the princes on 8th May after the majority had left Worms, the Diet being over. The Emperor in fact did not sign it himself until 26th May, though he dated it 8th, his intention being to give it the appearance of having been authorised by the full Diet, which in fact it was not. Luther returned to Wittemberg, thus, with the Pope's excommunication and the Imperial Edict of arrest hanging over him. How could he survive such immense forces? Yet the Lord was on his side and had prepared a way of escape. For as he passed through the Black Forest on 4th May, he was suddenly seized by masked armed horsemen, sent by friends, and mysteriously rushed away to a castle called the Wartburg, where he was dressed as a knight and given the name Knight George. When Luther looked from his room high up in the castle, on the morning after his 'arrest' he knew where he was, though on the previous day the horsemen had taken a very devious route to shake off pursuers. He was close to Eisenach, the scene of his schooldays and the home of Ursula Cotta who had befriended him when he was in need. He was in fact in the hands of friends. Outside in Germany and Europe no-one knew what had happened to him. As far as was known he had been captured by a mysterious group of horsemen and had completely disappeared. This was the Lord's way of preserving him from the Papacy and the Emperor. He was to stay in this castle lost to the outside world for nearly a year, leaving it eventually on 1st March, 1522 to return to Wittemberg. In this place he was to spend his time in rest which he needed so much after the strain of the years 1517-1521. Also he was to translate the New Testament from Greek to German. He began his translation in September 1521 and the first edition appeared in the same month of the following year. Thus was the Lord's hand seen and felt in the Reformation. "Out of weakness was made strong," was Luther's experience. The Lord's work was enhanced by the magnitude of the victory over such great enemies of the truth— "None can stay his hand or say unto him, What doest thou?"

In Wittemberg the leadership of the Reformation was taken over for the time by Carlstadt, who had spoken with Luther at Leipzig. He pressed on with reform so quickly, destroying images in churches and removing altars and changing the service of Communion from the Mass, that by December 1521 riots developed in many Churches in Wittemberg, some resisting his reforms. This concerned Luther very much. He secretly visited Wittemberg on one occasion and finally, the following March 1522, he felt he must take the risk and come out of his seclusion to deal with the disturbances. He saw that after so long a period of control, reform must progress slowly; that sincere Roman Catholics who did not agree with the reforms should not be rudely and roughly interfered with in their worship or the Reformation would get a bad name for using force. By now the Reformation teaching was so strong in the Elector of Saxony's Kingdom and the Elector favoured it to such an extent that Luther was comparatively safe, so long as he did not visit the state of a pro-Roman Catholic ruler. Also there were now many states in Germany whose rulers favoured the Reformation. This became clear at the Diet of Nürnberg held in March 1522 when the Diet refused to act on the Edict of Worms, and sent instead a list of grievances to the Pope which it wanted put right before it would act. While the Pope was considering them, the Diet gave permission for the Gospel to be freely preached in Germany by Luther and his followers.

In July 1523 the first martyrs of the Reformation were burnt at Brussels in Belgium. This was within the territory ruled by Charles V, but outside Germany. It showed what could have happened to Luther had not Charles V been opposed by the German princes. In April 1522 the Reformation had started in Switzerland at Zurich, when Zwingli had spoken out against some of the practices of the Catholic Church. Between 1523-4 Luther completed the first part of his translation of the Old Testament. Then in 1524 trouble started in Germany. Held for so long under the firm grip of the Roman Catholic Church, the newly found religious freedom and spirit of inquiry brought to Germany a social revolution. In that year the peasants rebelled in large numbers and burnt down many of the houses of the German nobility and captured several towns. There was much bloodshed before the rising was finally put down by the armies of the princes. The Roman Catholic Church tried to make out that the rising was the direct outcome of the Reformation teaching. Luther roundly condemned the peasants for using force and disassociated the Reformation from the revolt. It was a very embarrassing position for him, for he agreed with many of the grievances of the peasants and their desire for freedom and knew that the sight of the weakening of the Roman Catholic temporal supremacy in Germany had incited them to rebel against their feudal serfdom. But all his life, except in his stay at the Wartburg castle, when he was known as Knight George, Luther had refused to wear a sword and always resisted the idea of the princes defending the Reformation by force. After he died in 1546, the Protestant princes took up the sword and Germany was rent by the religious wars which Luther had always dreaded and tried to avert, and the Protestant-Roman Catholic struggle was not resolved finally in Germany for another century, until the Peace of Westphalia signed in 1648, by which both sides agreed to leave each other alone as neither could conquer the other.

In July 1524, a month after the start of the Peasants' Revolt, the Roman Catholic princes signed the Alliance of Regensberg with the intention of putting the Edict of Worms into practice and exterminating the Reformed 'heresy'. But they were unable to enforce their views without going to war and this they were not ready to do. In the following year, the Elector Frederick of Saxony, who had always supported Luther's cause, died and was succeeded as Elector by John the Steadfast. This man also took Luther's side and gave him as much support as his predecessor. In June 1525 Luther was married to Katherine von Bora, a lady who had once been a nun. In December he published his well-known book against free-will, called "Of Unfree will", or better known as "The Bondage of the Will." In these years from 1525-1529 the Emperor Charles V fought two wars against the French and so was not able to give much attention to the affairs of Germany. At the Diet of Speyer in 1526 it was agreed by the princes to adjourn the execution of the Edict of Worms until the matter could be more fully discussed. In 1529, when the Diet met again at Speyer, it was decided that in the States which had originally accepted the Edict of Worms, i.e. the Roman Catholic States, nothing could now be changed —the Mass could not be abolished, and no-one could embrace Reformed truths. In other words, the Diet tried to halt the spread of Reformed views in pro-Roman Catholic areas of Germany and so halt the Reformation from spreading any further. In face of this opposition, six of the princes and fourteen of the States and Cities of Germany who supported the Reformed position, issued a solemn *Protest* and so in course of time the followers of the Reformed Faith received the name *Protestants*.

In June 1530 the Imperial Diet opened at Augsburg and the two sides, Protestant and Roman Catholic, representing the various States of Germany, confronted each other in the German Parliament. At the time of the opening ceremony, when the Pope's delegate gave the benediction, the Emperor and Roman Catholic princes fell on their knees, but the Protestant princes stood erect and refused to bow. The Elector of Saxony, who was present, refused to take Luther with him for the sake of his safety. He left him in the castle at Coburg from April to October while the Diet debated and kept in constant touch with him. Luther gave advice to his supporters from a safe distance. An order was issued by the Diet that no Protestant ministers were to preach at Augsburg. On a protest from the Protestant princes it was agreed that no Roman Catholic clergy should preach either. In the name of the Protestant princes, Melanchthon, Luther's fellow Reformer, drew up a Confession of Faith which was read on 25th June before the Emperor and the whole Diet. When the reading of it started, the Protestant princes rose to signify their assent. The reading of it lasted two hours and was remarkable in that the Protestant cause was so fully and clearly stated in public. This statement of faith, since called. "The Augsburg Confession," was the equivalent for the Lutheran Church in Germany of the 39 Articles for the Church of England. It contained twenty-eight articles. Later the Roman Catholics produced a Confession and it also was read before the Diet.

The differences were now crystal clear between the Roman Catholics and the Protestants and it was obvious to both sides that there could be no reconciliation. The Roman Catholics in the Diet proceeded to pass a decree which almost amounted to a prohibition of religious liberty in Germany. This alarmed

MARTIN LUTHER

the Protestant princes and they met at Smalkalden in December 1530 after the Diet of Augsburg was over to sign a treaty of mutual defence against all aggressors and called for help from the Kings of France and England. Luther was very hesitant about taking such action. He entirely disagreed with the use of force and felt it was wrong for the Protestant cause to depend for its existence on the use of force. Yet the fact remained that if it had not been for the support of these men and their armies the Protestant cause would have been subject to some very bitter persecution in Germany in Luther's lifetime, whereas under this shield it was allowed to grow.

So the years passed by—in 1534 Luther completed his translation of the Old Testament and the first complete edition of the German Bible was published. In 1539 the first volume of Luther's complete works, the Wittemberg Edition, was published. In 1543 printing started on Luther's great work on Genesis, the result of lectures given between 1535-1545. On 13th December, 1545 the Council of Trent opened its discussions—this was the great Roman Catholic Church Council which was to deal with the rift caused by the Reformation, examine the causes and produce what historians have since called 'The Counter-Reformation.' Luther was not to live to see it accomplish its work. He died while staying at Eisleben, his birthplace, on 18th February, 1546 and his body was taken back to Wittemberg and buried there on 22nd February. Thus died "the monk that shook the world."